Scholastic Children's Books,
Euston House, 24 Eversholt Street,
London, NW1 1DB, UK

A division of Scholastic Ltd
London ~ New York ~ Toronto ~ Sydney ~ Auckland
Mexico City ~ New Delhi ~ Hong Kong

Published by Scholastic Ltd, 2015

CONTENTS

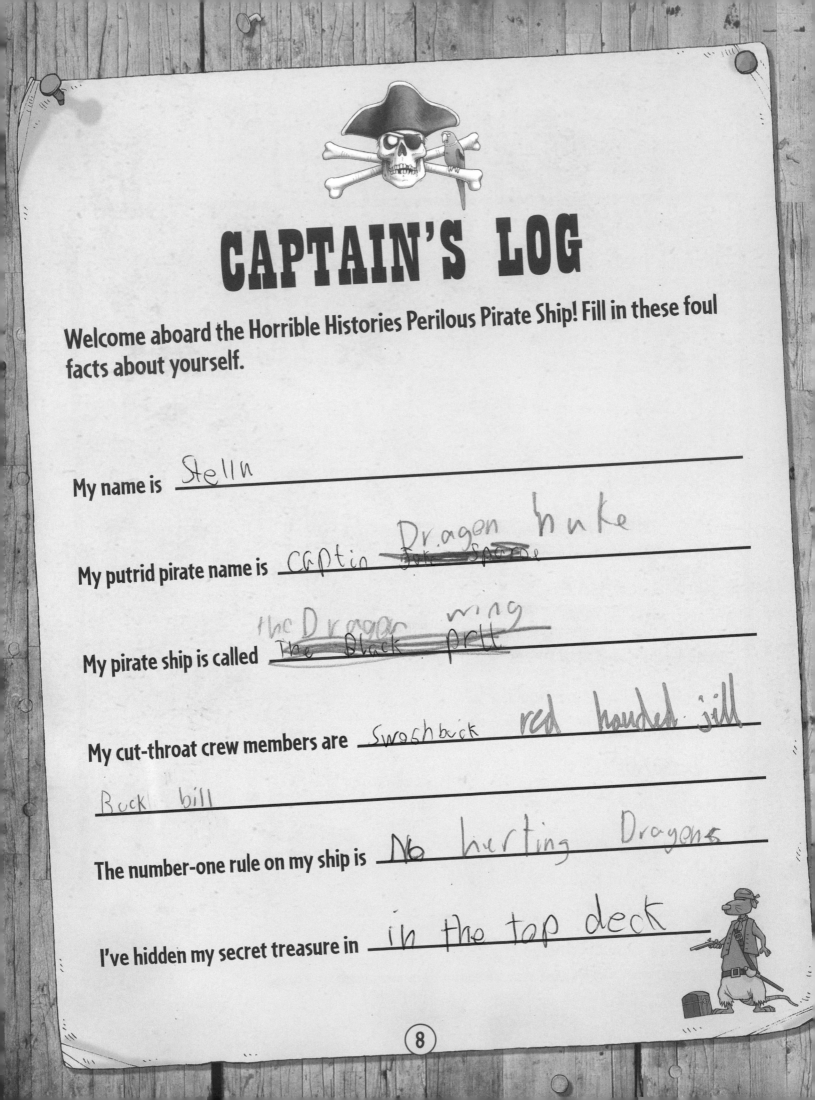

CAPTAIN'S LOG

Welcome aboard the Horrible Histories Perilous Pirate Ship! Fill in these foul facts about yourself.

My name is Stella

My putrid pirate name is captin Dragon Dork sparrow nuke

My pirate ship is called the Dragon wing The black prll

My cut-throat crew members are Swoshbck red handed jill Buck bill

The number-one rule on my ship is No hurting Dragons

I've hidden my secret treasure in in the top deck

Draw yourself as a putrid pirate complete with deadly pirate flag.

HORRIBLE HENGE

Everyone has heard of Stonehenge – those creepy-looking stones in Wiltshire have been around since prehistoric times. There have been some strange ideas throughout the ages about what they were used for, but which one of these weird and wacky theories is true?

A

STONEHENGE IS ABOUT THE SAME AGE AS THE PYRAMIDS, SO IT MUST HAVE BEEN BUILT BY EGYPTIANS

PROFESSOR E.X. PERT

B

STONEHENGE WAS BUILT BY PRIESTS FROM A MEDITERRANEAN ISLAND IN 1600 BC

PROFESSOR BRIAN STORM

C

OCH AYE! I HAVE PROVED THAT STONEHENGE IS THE SITE OF THE GARDEN OF EDEN. THE WORLD STARTED HERE!

SCOT McNUTTER

D

STONEHENGE WAS BUILT BY ALIENS AS A LAUNCH PAD FOR THEIR SPACE SHIPS

N.E. JIT

Answer: None!

Archaeologists can explain how Stonehenge was built in the days before cranes and bulldozers. They've experimented with raising stones using ropes and wood. They can tell you *when* it was built and show how it used to look. But they *can't* agree on what happened inside the stone circle. Guess it'll have to remain a mystery for now then.

Stonehenge is not the only stone circle in the British Isles – they are everywhere. Many stone-circle legends say the stones were once people or animals. Others say the stones were...

A complete wedding party, turned to stone for dancing on a Sunday (Stanton Drew, Avon, England)

Three women who sinned by working on a Sunday (Moelfre Hill, Wales)

Giants who refused to be christened when Christianity came to the land (Western Isles of Scotland)

Women who gave false evidence that led to a man being hanged (Cottrell, South Wales)

A girl running away from a wizard who wanted to marry her (Aberdeen, Scotland)

A cow, a witch and a fisherman (Inisbofin, Ireland)

A giant and his seven sons who went to war with a wizard (Kerry, Ireland)

A mermaid's children (Cruckancornia, Ireland)

Lots of places said the stones were robbers caught stealing from churches, or history teachers who gave impossibly hard homework and were turned to stone by pupils with witch powers ... you wish!

THIS IS SO UNFAIR. LOOK AT THE SIZE OF THE STONE I'VE BEEN TURNED INTO – IT'S HUGE. WHAT'S EVERYONE GOING TO THINK? I WAS NEVER THAT FAT!

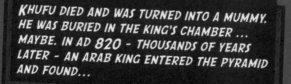

KHUFU DIED AND WAS TURNED INTO A MUMMY. HE WAS BURIED IN THE KING'S CHAMBER ... MAYBE. IN AD 820 - THOUSANDS OF YEARS LATER - AN ARAB KING ENTERED THE PYRAMID AND FOUND...

HUGE BLOCKS OF STONE FILLED THE PASSAGEWAY. THIEVES HAD NOT BROKEN IN, YET THE COFFIN WAS EMPTY AND...

THIS COFFIN IS TOO SMALL TO HOLD A CORPSE ANYWAY ... UNLESS THE LEGS ARE BENT

NOTHING!

4

Tomb builders, guards and priests could all help with a robbery. Promise to give them a share of the loot and they will let you rob the grave and get away. In the end the Egyptians saw that pyramids didn't work. They started burying their kings in tombs dug into the rock – a new graveyard called 'The Valley of the Kings'.

In AD 1301 an earthquake shook all the bright white stones off the Great Pyramid of Khufu. The pyramid you can see today is not the smooth and gleaming tomb that Khufu had built.

PESKY KIDS

BUFF

BRRRMMM

WHEEEE!

ISN'T IT A TOUCH OSTENTATIOUS?

LOOKS IMPRESSIVE

BUFF

NOT FROM WHERE I'M STANDING

PHARAOH NUFF'S PYRAMID PAPYRUS WEIGHTS

SOLD

MAKE YOURSELF AT HOME, MY LORD

CHIP
CHIP

SCRAPE

YOU CAN TAKE THAT BACK, BOYS – IT'S FINISHED

HANG ON, I'M NOT DEAD YET!

THAT COULD BE ARRANGED

ROTTEN ROMAN ARMY

In the year AD 43 the Romans invaded Britain. The Roman Army didn't run all of Roman Britain. Once they'd won the battles they moved on to fight somewhere else. Towns were built in the beaten bits with Roman lords in charge.

Your teachers will tell you all about the legions and what they wore and how they lived. But they don't know everything.

TEST YOUR TEACHER...

Test your knowledge of what life was really like in the rotten Roman Army. You'll find the answers on page 56.

If you were a Roman soldier...

1 What would you wear under your leather kilt?
a) nothing
b) underpants
c) fig leaves

2 Where would you drive on the Roman roads?
a) on the right
b) down the centre
c) on the left

I'M A
CENTURIAN
CENTURIAN

3 How long would you have to stay in the army once you joined?
a) 25 years
b) 5 years
c) the rest of your life

4 Who could you marry?
a) your granny
b) no one
c) a Roman

5 Who paid for your uniform, weapons, food and burial?
a) the emperor
b) your granny
c) you paid for them yourself out of your wages

6 How tall did you have to be?
a) over 1.8 metres
b) between 1.6 and 1.8 metres
c) tall enough to touch your toes

7 What would you use instead of toilet paper?
a) a sponge on the end of a stick
b) your tunic
c) the daily newspaper

8 Your spear (pilum) had a 60 cm metal head that would snap off after it hit something. Why?
a) so the enemy couldn't pick up the spear and throw it back
b) so you could put the metal head in your pocket when you were marching
c) because the Roman armourers couldn't make the heads stay on

9 Why was one Roman Centurion called "Give me another"?
a) because he liked his soldiers to sing as they marched. When they'd finished one song he'd call out, "Give me another!"
b) because he was greedy. After eating a pig's head he'd cry out, "Give me another!"
c) because he cruelly beat his soldiers so hard he smashed his canes and had to call out "Give me another!"

"GIVE ME ANOTHER!"

10 Why would the army doctor not notice your screams as he treated your wounds?
a) because he enjoyed making you suffer
b) because he was trained to carry on without caring about a soldier's cries
c) because the Romans only employed deaf men as doctors

CELTIC COMPASS GAMES

Did you know that the Celts were skilful sailors? They needed a good sense of direction – after all, they didn't want to sail over the edge of the world which (as we can all see) is flat. But the Celtic sailors didn't describe directions as North, South, East or West. They used colours. The sun rose in the 'purple' and by midday was in the 'white'. You too could become a geographical genius by learning this chart...

Celt compass games
Of course simply learning these directions is no fun. You have to use them. Try giving someone directions using the Celtic compass...

Game I
You'll need:
- ten or more players
- four signs saying North, South, East and West.

All you do is:

1 Place the cards on each of the four walls of a large room or hall.

2 There is one 'caller' and the rest are runners.

3 The caller selects a colour – say, 'white' – and shouts it.

4 The players have to run to the correct sign – in this case 'South'.

SHARON'S ALWAYS BEEN VERY COMPETITIVE AT GAMES

5 The last one to touch the South wall Is out.

6 The game continues with one player dropping out each round. Obviously, the corners are the colours or shades between the main compass points. 'Dark' or 'speckled' means North-east.

7 The winner is the last player in. Change callers and start again.

8 When the players are getting faster then add a new call … 'Cut-throat!' This means 'Freeze'. Everyone who moves after the call is out.

Game 2

You'll need:
- at least two players
- a room full of obstructions (like chairs)
- a scarf for a blindfold.

All you do is:

1 The aim is for the leader to get the blindfolded partner safely across the room to a target without bumping, breaking or even touching an obstruction in between. (It would also be nice if the blindfolded partner does not break a leg.)

2 The leader must talk the partner through the obstacles but can only use the Celt compass to do so.

3 'Black' becomes straight ahead, 'white' is backwards, 'purple' is right and 'pale' is left. 'Dark brown' is a little to the left and 'grey' is more to the left and so on.

4 The leader cannot use the word 'Stop' (or left, right, ahead or back) but they can add the word 'Cut-throat!' meaning 'Stop!'

5 Score 10 for a clear run to the target; deduct a point for every obstacle touched.

6 Change the blindfold to the leader and try again. The winner is the one with the highest score as leader.

7 If there is more than one pair, then the pairs can race from one end of the room to the other. Touching any obstacle means the pair must go back to the start.

8 The winner is the pair to reach the far wall first. In the event of a tie the winner is the blindfolded partner with the fewest broken bones.

NASTY NORMANS

The Battle of Hastings took place in 1066, when fierce Norman, Duke William I, invaded the south coast of England to fight English King Harold in battle. (Wicked William won, becoming William the Conqueror.)

It's England's most famous battle, but how much do you know about it? Just answer True or False...

1 William fell in the sea when he landed. True or False?
2 Before the battle William put on his chain mail back to front. True or False?
3 William wore a rabbit's foot for luck. True or False?
4 The Norman attack was led by a juggler. True or False?
5 The English were packed so tight that the dead and wounded couldn't fall to the ground. True or False?
6 William was known as 'the Conqueror' because he liked playing conkers. True or False?
7 King Harold was killed with an arrow in his eye. True or False?
8 The Normans knew they'd killed Harold because he wore a crown. True or False?
9 The Normans said they buried Harold under a rose bush. True or False?
10 The English said Harold DIDN'T die at Hastings. True or False?

CASTLE CURIOSITIES

Lords in Norman times were nervous. They had just a few knights to keep those thousands of English peasants pleasant. If the English rebelled then there would be b-i-g trouble. So, just to be on the safe side, the Normans built whacking great castles. The terrible towers gave a message to the pitiful peasants...

1

Don't even THINK about rebelling!

But they were NOT the most comfortable places to live. Cold and damp in winter, then in the summer they were ... well, cold and damp. As for the toilets! You do NOT want to know about the toilets. You do? Oh, very well, read on. YOU asked for it...

Messy moats

A castle was often built with a band of water round the outside so attackers couldn't put ladders down. But all the toilets emptied into the moat and it soon began to fill up with human waste and smelled like a dead rat's gut. If you fell in you might not drown – but you would be poisoned if you swallowed any water.

FANCY A SWIM?

24

2 Fishy flavour

The moats were often filled with fish. The castle cooks would have the fish caught and serve them up for dinner. But would YOU want to feast on fish that fed on filth?

Gooey garderobes

The posh people in the castle had their own toilet rooms called garderobes – because that's where they guarded robes: kept their clothes. Why keep their best clothes in the toilet? Because moths like to lay their eggs in clothes and when the eggs hatch out with grubs they eat holes in the clothes. Hang your clothes in the toilet and the moths will keep away – they can't stand the smell.

Shmelly shafts

A toilet was often just a hole in the floor. Under the hole was a stone shaft that led down into the toilet pit below (or into the moat if you had one).

The trouble is, attackers could sometimes climb up this shaft and get into your castle. If you were REALLY unlucky you could be sitting on the toilet seat when they popped up!

WHO'S UNLUCKY?

Ashes to ashes

If you are at a feast you do NOT want to miss the tasty treats and the brilliant booze for a moment. So you would NOT want to say, 'Excuse me while I pop out to the little boys' (or girls') room!' and then wander down dark corridors looking for a loo, getting lost and cold and hungry. No, you would go to the fireplace in the dining hall and widdle in the ashes. Sizzle and hiss.

Putrid pits

Not every castle had a moat. Those castles without had a toilet pit or 'cesspit' where all the poo collected. Of course it would begin to fill up. You needed someone to empty it with shovels, fill up wheelbarrows with it and cart it off. Would YOU like that wheely nice job? The men who did it were called 'gong farmers'. The waste could be spread over the fields to make the crops grow!

HORRIBLE HISTORIES HINT:
If you ever meet a gong farmer, try not to shake hands with him.

GOING GOING GONG.

Bum job

The lords and knights of the castle didn't want to wander to the toilet shaft in the garderobe in the middle of the night. They used a potty set into a chair – known as a 'stool'. A servant would empty it in the morning. If you think THAT'S a bad job then you will feel sorry for the servant of monster knight, Henry VIII. The servant's job was to follow Henry to the toilet and wipe his fat backside.

Terrific toilets

If you were on guard duty up on the castle walls, then you would not walk down for a midnight pee. You would just widdle over the wall.

Mopping-up job

NOT THE CURTAINS!

Paper was expensive and hard to make in the Middle Ages. No one would use it for toilet paper. Instead you'd use a bit of straw or moss. Posh people might use a damp cloth. What did most knights use? Nothing.

Lousy leather

Often there were workshops inside the castle walls, including one for a 'tanner' – a man who took the skin of a cow and turned it into leather for jackets and shoes. He softened up the skin by putting it in a barrel with lots of juicy dog-poo and trampling it. Nice.

TOXIC TANNER

PONGY GONG FARMER

SPLISHY SPLOSHY

DID YOU KNOW...?
Stairways in castle towers go up clockwise. Why? If someone is chasing you up a castle tower then it is easier for a right-handed swordsman to back up the stairs. A right-handed attacker would find it difficult to chase after him. BUT some castles, like Caerphilly in Wales, have a couple of stairways that go up anti-clockwise. If you find you are fighting to get into your own tower then you would choose one of those!

GOOD BOY

SUFFERING SCHOOLS

In the Middle Ages in England and Wales it was tough at school.

Schools – the good news

✤ You didn't have to go if you were poor ... or a girl.

✤ Most boys only went to school from the ages of 7 to 14.

✤ There was no homework.

✤ There were no spelling corrections – you spelled English any way you wanted to.

Schools – the bad news

✤ You had no break-times – only a short stop for lunch.

✤ Make a mistake and you were beaten – usually with branches from a birch tree.

✤ You had to buy your own paper, ink and books – which were very expensive.

✤ And of course there were 'School Rules'…

Westminster School in the 13th century had the following rules…

Let them say prayers every morning without shouting

Let there be no grinning or chattering or laughing

Let them not make fun of another if he does not read or sing well

Let them not hit one another secretly

Let them not answer rudely if questioned by their elders

LET THOSE WHO BREAK THESE RULES FEEL THE ROD WITHOUT DELAY!

Not too bad so far? Not much different from your own school, apart from the bit about being hit with a rod!

Some of the other rules were really odd. But they must have needed these rules because someone actually did these dreadful deeds…

Anyone who has torn to pieces his school mate's bed or hidden the bedclothes or thrown shoes or pillow from corner to corner or thrown the school into disorder shall be severely punished in the morning.

No wonder this boy's 15th-century poem was so popular with pupils. He wrote about being late for school and giving a cheeky reply to his teacher…

My master looks like he is mad,
'Where have you been, my sorry lad?'
'Milking ducks my mother had!'
It is no wonder that I'm sad.

My master peppered my backside with speed,
It was worse than fennel seed;
He would not stop till it did bleed,
I'm truly sorry for his deed.

I wish my master was a hare,
And all his fat books hound dogs were.
Me, the hunter, I'd not spare
Him. If he died I would not care!

Why was the boy late? You might well ask. Well, school often began at five in the morning in summer time! Wouldn't you be late?

LOST PRUPERTY

Shoe
Sports kit socks

MUCKY MANNERS

Young people in the Middle Ages had books to teach them table manners. Unfortunately not a lot of young people could read. It may have been better to have had illustrations to help. Draw lines to match the putrid picture to the instruction it goes with. Number 2 is completed to show you how it's done.

1. DO NOT clean your nails or your teeth with your eating knife.

2. DO NOT wipe your knife on the tablecloth.

3. DO NOT play with the tablecloth or blow your nose on your napkin.

4. DO NOT dip your bread in the soup.

5. DO NOT fill your soup spoon too full or blow on your soup.

6. DO NOT eat noisily or clean your bowl by licking it out.

7. DO NOT speak while your mouth is full of food.

8. DO NOT spit over the table but spit on the floor.

9. DO NOT tear at meat but cut it with a knife first.

10. DO NOT take the best food for yourself. Share it.

A

B

C

D

E

F

G

H

I

J

GRUESOME GRID

Copy the Middle Ages rat into the squares.

SCRAMBLED SAYINGS

The Irish, Scots and Welsh all have their own languages. But most people in Britain speak English most of the time.

They use the English language to say some pretty potty things – and some curiously clever things if you think about them.

Take the Irish in the Middle Ages. They had some puzzling sayings, like 'It's a bad hen that won't scratch herself' meaning people should be able to do their own work. That's useful when your mother tells you to go to the shop or do the washing up. (But not when your pocket money depends on it.)

Now you've got the idea, you should have no trouble putting the two halves of these Irish proverbs back together. Match the first column with the last. (Work out what they mean – or simply go around saying them, and everyone will think you're brilliant!)

1 a woman's tongue

2 death

3 the mouth of the grave

4 a trout in the pot

5 even a tin knocker

6 between two blind goats it

7 any man

8 when the tongue slips it

a) speaks the truth

b) is difficult to choose

c) is better than a salmon in the sea

d) can lose his hat in a fairy wind

e) does not rust

f) is the poor man's doctor

g) will shine on a dirty door

h) gives to the needy one

Answers on page 57

ROLAND'S ROTTEN END
15 AUGUST, AD 778

WHAT IS A KNIGHT? IT'S A NOBLE MAN ON A HORSE, WHOSE JOB IS TO KILL HIS ENEMIES. BUT IT IS MORE THAN THAT. THE KNIGHT HAS 'RULES' CALLED CHIVALRY. CHIVALRY MEANS HE CAN DO DAFT THINGS ... LIKE FIGHT TO THE DEATH TO SAVE HIS FRIENDS. WHERE DID THESE 'RULES' COME FROM? FROM STORIES. TRUE TALES OF HEROES OR MADE-UP TALES. OTHER KNIGHTS HEARD THE STORIES THEN SAID, 'OOOOH! THAT'S WHAT WE SHOULD BE DOING.' STORIES ABOUT KNIGHTS LIKE ROLAND...

1

KING CHARLES THE GREAT OF FRANCE (SOMETIMES CALLED CHARLEMAGNE) WAS ... GREAT.

I'M GREAT, I AM. ME AND MY KNIGHTS ARE UNBEATABLE. KNIGHTS LIKE ROLAND HERE

ME, AND MY TRUSTY SWORD CALLED DURENDAL

I'M A LORD'S SWORD - A CUT ABOVE THE REST

NOT TO MENTION MY FAITHFUL HORSE, VEILLANTIF

I'M THE MANE REASON FOR HIS SUCCESS

HUH! ROLAND SAID NOT TO MENTION YOU

NO, NO! WE JUST SORT OF ... DIDN'T WIN

BUT YOU CAPTURED LOTS OF LOVELY LOOT, MY NOBLE KING

AS IF A HEAVY HORSEMAN AND HIS SWORD WASN'T ENOUGH TO CARRY? BAGS OF GOLD TOO

WE REACHED A HIGH MOUNTAIN PASS ON THE ROAD BACK TO FRANCE...

HEAVY HORSEMAN, SWORD, BAGS OF GOLD **AND** MOUNTAINS TO CLIMB!

WHINNY, WHINNY, WHINGE - THAT'S ALL YOU EVER DO

AND THAT'S WHERE WE RAN INTO TROUBLE...

WE ARE IN THE LAND OF THE BASQUES, MY LORD. DANGEROUS FIGHTERS

BIG BAD BASQUES MAKE OLLY LESS JOLLY

'The Song of Roland' is the oldest French tale around. It was written 500 years after the battle where Roland died, so it isn't all true. The story would have been sung by travelling poets – 'troubadours', the French called them. The knights would hear the poems and get the idea, 'That's how a good knight behaves!' There is a tombstone near the Roncevaux Pass showing the area where it is thought Roland died. One story says Roland was chopped down by a child. The killer kid, Iñigo Arista, went on to be first king of Navarre in Northern Spain. A boy who butchered big bold Roland? Believe it if you like.

4

TERRIFYING TUDOR DRESS-UP

Transform Rattus into different terrible Tudors with these outfits. Just follow the instructions below (you might want an adult to help you with the fiddly and sharp bits).

1. Cut out pages 35 and 37 of this annual, or make a colour photocopy if you don't want to damage the paper.

2. Roughly cut around each figure of Rattus and stick them on separate pieces of card (or one piece of card, but with lots of space in between them).

3. When the glue is dry, carefully cut around each figure of Rattus and fold the stand back where shown.

4. Cut around the Tudor outfits and glue them carefully to the Rattus figures.

5. Stand back and admire your horrible creations. You could even hide them around the house to scare family members...

Elizabeth I

fold

fold

Mary I

fold

fold

SPOT THE LOT!

Can you spot all ten differences between these two pictures of Charles II?

PERILOUS PIRATE TIMELINE

Want to learn more about those putrid pirates who ruled the waves and struck fear in the hearts of whoever they met? To give you a rough idea of who was doing what and when, here is a quick timeline...

Around 1100 BC The first pirates roam the Mediterranean seas.

230 BC Queen Teuta of Illyria (that's Albania today) is fed up with the Greeks settling on the coast of her country. She hasn't the forces to drive them out of their towns so she turns pirate to sink them at sea. But when she tries to be ruthless with Roman ships she is defeated.

Vikings cross the North Sea and slaughter monks.

AD 401 St Patrick (AD 385–461) was a British boy who was taught the Bible by his dad. When St Pat was sixteen he was captured by pirates and sold as a slave in Ireland. After six years he escaped to Gaul (now France) and became a monk. He then went BACK to Ireland and converted the Irish to Christianity. If the pirates hadn't sent him to Ireland he might never have become their greatest saint.

Don't be surprised. Scramble the letters of 'pirates' and you get 'a priest'.

AD 793 It's the start of the Viking age. They will spill blood on land and sea for more than three hundred years.

1492 Christopher Columbus discovers the West Indies and finds that the Arawak Indians make great slaves. He starts the slave trade that has traders crossing the Atlantic to make their fortunes – and pirates to pinch it.

1500s The Barbarossa brothers, Aruj and Kheir-ed-din, roam the Mediterranean. The name means 'Red beard', which is better than being called 'Green beard'. These corsairs were feared throughout the Mediterranean for their vicious attacks on Christian ships and towns.

1603 England stops allowing her 'privateers' to attack foreign ships, but the English sailors carry on the raids anyway against the law. These are the days of the buccaneers in the Caribbean.

1618 There are now about 5,000 pirates at sea – mostly in the Caribbean. There's a great trade there in slaves and sugar plus lots of lovely hiding places thousands of miles from the nasty navies. A pirate paradise in fact.

1697 Treaty of Ryswick. Spain, France, Holland and England agree to stop privateers raiding each other's ships. Pirates can no longer say, 'I was fighting for my country,' and get away with it. A caught pirate is a dead pirate from now on. Just to prove it the English hang Captain Kidd in 1701.

1775 The Americans are in revolt against Britain. American ships start to attack and rob British ships. John Paul Jones makes a daring raid on Britain and becomes an American hero. The Brits just see him as a pirate.

1850s Steam-powered ships make it easier to catch pirates. There are only a few pirate crews left now. The seas are a bit safer.

WICKED WEAPONS

If you want to be a pirate you need to have plenty of weapons. You will want to stab, shoot, smash down doors, chop through ropes and burn sails. Here are some usual – and unusual – weapons for you to wear.

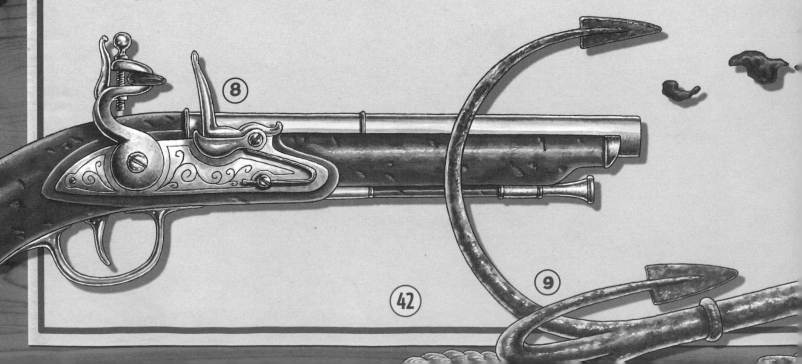

1. Cutlass

Why did pirates like the curvy 'cutlass' sword? Because there were lots of ropes on a sailing ship. The curved sword didn't get tangled in the ropes. Unless you used it the wrong way round, of course...

2. Brass knife

Salty water makes iron and steel rot and rust. A brass knife would stay sharp. It was usually short and sharp for cutting and stabbing. (It is also useful for picking your teeth if you've forgotten to pack your corsair toothbrush. Just don't use it to pick your nose.)

3. Axe

If you want an enemy ship to stop then chop the ropes that hold up the sails. The sails will collapse and fall on the crew. Pirate axes were around 70 cm long and weighed about a kilo. An axe is useful for a quick chop. And a quick chop is very nice – especially if it's a lamb chop.

4. Duck's foot

If you want to shoot someone use a duck's foot. This was a pistol with FOUR barrels. You could fire all four at the same time so you were sure to hit something. The barrels were joined together and looked a little like a duck's foot. You'd be quackers not to use one!

5. Tar bomb

Wrap a lump of tar, the size of your head, around a rope. When the enemy is close, set fire to the tar and use the rope to throw it on to the enemy deck or sails. It will stick and set fire to their ship. They won't be able to pull it off. While the crew try to put out the fire you jump aboard and attack them. Just make sure you don't step on one of your own tar bombs when you leap aboard.

6. Marlin spikes

These metal spikes with handles were not meant to be weapons but tools for working on ropes.

7. Buccaneer knives

Buccaneers in the Caribbean enjoyed hunting wild pigs or boars. They were expert shots but DIDN'T use their guns to kill the pigs. They enjoyed the 'sport' of running after the boar and chopping it down with their long sharp knives. Each buccaneer had at least two large knives. These knives were shorter than a cutlass. The aim was to slice the back legs of the pig so it couldn't run. They would then jump it from behind and slit its throat.

8. Flintlock pistols

These pistols were used by Caribbean pirates but they weren't deadly. They were noisy and made clouds of smoke but were not very accurate. They took a long time to load and often didn't fire at all. Pirates like Blackbeard carried a dozen of them stuffed into his belt to save time. One of them would work sooner or later – or you could always throw them at your enemy.

9. Grappling hooks

Iron hooks on the end of a long rope. Throw them across to an enemy ship and pull on the rope. The other ship won't be able to sail away from you. It's a bit like a spider trapping a fly.

...and one weapon to use AGAINST a pirate attack:

10. Cows

In 1670 Panama City was under attack. The Spanish governor wasn't too worried because he had a secret weapon ... a herd of cows, trained to charge at the English enemy.

The English were led by the famous Welsh pirate, Sir Henry Morgan. His men were exhausted. On the march to Panama they were so starved they had to eat their own boots. Morgan's men charged. The Spanish set the cows loose ... but they were scared by the pirates. They turned around and charged the Spanish by mistake. Oo-oops! (Or should that be moo-oops?) The Spanish fled but burned the city so Morgan went back with nothing. Still, at least they had cows to eat. Tastier than boots.

YUM!

WHICH PERILOUS PIRATE ARE YOU?

Which dastardly member of the high seas are you? Take the quiz and find out, if you dare...

Are you good at staying away from things that are bad for you?

Black, the colour of night.

What is your battle colour of choice?

Red, the colour of blood.

Of course! But no one is fast enough to catch me...

Are you likely to hold a grudge?

Are you prepared to die in battle?

No chance! I'd rather surrender and live, thanks.

They're crusty old spoilsports out to ruin my fun.

How do you feel about royalty?

They're great! They're always getting me out of sticky situations.

What do you value most?

I pride myself on my great restraint. It keeps me sharp, focused and deadly.

You're BLACK BART (BARTHOLOMEW ROBERTS)
Rising from being an officer on board a slave ship that got captured to ruling the seas on a gigantic ship of your own, you're a true self-starter. Your ruthlessness, determination and love of power mean you steal the most loot, which makes you the most successful pirate out there. Take that, Blackbeard!

No, not if it stops me enjoying myself.

You're BLACKBEARD (EDWARD TEACH)
Your reputation precedes you. Known for your black hair plaited with snakes, you've even occasionally put candles in the plaits before battle to seem more intimidating. You and your sinister ship *Queen Anne's Revenge,* are feared throughout the waves – no one wants to encounter you!

No. I hate everyone anyway whether they've done something wrong or not.

You're NED (EDWARD) LOW
Wow, those who upset you don't fare well, do they? You grew up rough, and became strong and scary with a reputation for cruelty (you once made a prisoner eat the heart of his friend, ouch). It's safe to say you're not the most popular person around – your own crew eventually set you adrift in a tiny boat – but it's better to be feared than loved, right?

Yes – I always tend to focus my anger on one person.

You're JEANNE DE CLISSON
Also known as the Lioness of Brittany, you're a formidable pirate who pursued French King Philip VI across the English Channel, destroying his ships and killing his men to avenge your husband (who Philip executed). With your single-mindedness and dedication to the art of getting even, people wouldn't want to get on your bad side!

Fame and respect – I love everyone knowing my name.

You're HENRY MORGAN
Coming from a wealthy background, you took to the seas for some raiding, yet also managed to keep your powerful friends and be knighted in England rather than being hanged for your crimes. Things always seem to work out well for you, except for that time a sailor knocked a candle onto gunpowder and blew up your ship...

Jewels and silver. Who wouldn't want to be rich?

You're LADY MARY KILLIGREW
Silver and jewels are your main priority, and you'll do whatever you can to get them. You're also a crafty pirate, burying treasure in your garden to stop it being stolen. You nearly get hanged, but good old Queen Liz likes you so you just get a jail sentence. Aren't you popular!

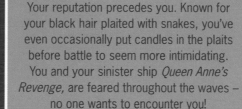

SPOT THE LOT!

Can you spot eight differences between these two pictures of beastly Blackbeard?

46

AWESOME ANNUAL WINNERS

In last year's annual we asked you to submit potty poems about a historical event or person. You rotten readers did not disappoint – there were tons of gruesomely gory limericks and ruthless rhymes submitted. Congratulations to our horrible winners, we've printed your entries below!

There once was a Viking called Thor,
Who was an incredible bore.
No pillage or burning,
He just had a yearning,
To lie in his longboat and snore!

Ben, age 7

We hold the skull and bones up high,
To let you know the end is nigh.
Don't tangle with this deadly crew,
'Cos we'll make mincemeat outta you!

Mohammed, age 14

There was a man called Tom,
Who went off to fight in the Somme.
There were rats in the trenches,
And terrible stenches,
And the sound of the mortar bombs.

Grace, age 8

PUTRID PRIZES

Find out what horrible prizes are in store for our wicked winners this year...

First prize

One lucky Horrible Histories fan is going to win a very Horrible prize – **a year's subscription** to the official Horrible Histories magazine! The magazine, which is in shops every month, is packed with cruel quizzes, foul fun, putrid puzzles and posters, wicked competitions and loads more from the bestselling books and CBBC TV show. Plus, each issue comes with crazy free gifts and a stack of savage stickers. So if you're a real fan, you'll definitely want to get your horrible hands on this magazine every month.

As if that wasn't enough, you'll also win a copy of a brand new Horrible Histories book: *Top 50 Kings & Queens* and a *Horrible Histories: The Specials* DVD.

Runners up

Three runners up will receive a whole collection of Horrible things, including either a Boudica or Blackbeard costume, a limited edition Horrible Histories Monopoly game, a copy of *Top 50 Kings & Queens* and a *Horrible Histories: The Specials* DVD.

To be in with a chance of winning, simply send us your own **Horrible Histories joke**. Entries should be about any historical person or event you've read about in this annual. The winning jokes will be published in the Horrible Histories Annual 2017!

Send your entry to:
Horrible Histories Annual 2016 Competition
Scholastic Children's Books
Euston House
24 Eversholt Street
London
NW1 1DB

Don't forget to add your name, age, address and postcode to the back of the entry, so that we know where to send the prizes. Please get your parent or guardian to sign the back of your entry before you put it into an envelope. Please also state whether you'd like to recieve a **Boudica costume** or a **Blackbeard costume**.

The competition closes on 13th April 2016. Winning entrants will be notified within 28 days of the closing date.

Savage small-print

BOMB SPOTTING

Know your enemy, they say. So if you want to survive the Blitz get to know these blitzing bombs.

If you are close enough to spot a bomb then you'll probably be dead a few seconds later. So spot these bombs ... then duck!

High explosive
A big bang that blasts down walls, wrecks water pipes, gas pipes and electric cables and makes holes in the road so rescue vehicles can't get to the fires and the victims.

Magnesium incendiary bombs
They land and start burning fiercely. Very hard to put out the fires.

Petrol incendiary bombs
Spread flaming petrol over a wide area so there's less chance of escape.

High-explosive parachute air-mines
They float down, explode in the air and blow the roofs off buildings. That way the next lot of incendiary bombs will fall INSIDE buildings, not just on the roof tiles.

Petrol incendiary parachute air-mines
Float down and spray flaming petrol on the buildings, people, cars (and cats and dogs) below.

Flares
They float slowest of all and burn brightly. Enemy aircrafts can see them from miles away and the light shows them where to drop their bombs.

V1 flying bomb
The 'Vergeltung' 1 bomb ... and that means 'Revenge'. It flies off a sort of ski-slope launcher.

V2 rocket bomb
Bigger, faster and nastier than the V1. They go 50 miles high so there's no stopping them.

INCENDIARY BOMB

PARACHUTE AIR-MINE

V1 FLYING BOMB

V2 FLYING BOMB

DAD'S ARMY

Men over 40 who were too old to join the army in WW2 formed a Home Guard in case Hitler's army invaded Britain. They were originally known as Local Defence Volunteers, but everyone called them Dad's Army.

Some things no one tells you about Dad's Army are...

1 War starts and Dad's Army have no weapons – the real army need them. So people with guns at home hand them over... One man says he is fighting with a gun from 1880.

I'VE A SHOTGUN I USE FOR PIGEONS

I'VE GOT A CAP GUN I USE TO SHOOT MY SISTER!

I HAVE A PISTOL FROM THE LAST WAR

2 They still don't have enough weapons so they go on parade with...

| Pickaxes | Coshes | Spears | Dummy wooden rifles | |

Then Winston Churchill says...

EVERY MAN MUST HAVE A WEAPON – EVEN IF IT IS ONLY A PIKE

Pikes were axes on long poles used in the Middle Ages. Churchill didn't MEAN it. But someone orders metal poles with daggers on the end and a quarter of a million are made.

Dad's Army are furious ... they make them look a bit of a joke. Very few of the new 'pikes' ever leave the factory.

3 You may think the Nazi invaders would treat the LDV as a joke. You're wrong! When Adolf Hitler hears about Dad's Army he rants…

LDV? They are murder gangs! When we invade they will be rounded up and executed.

Dad's Army must be pleased to know Adolf is so afraid of them!

4 The LDV learn to make their own weapons. Weapons like petrol bombs.

TODAY I'M GOING TO SHOW YOU HOW TO MAKE A PETROL BOMB WITH A BEER BOTTLE AND SOME PETROL…

FIRST DRINK THE BEER … I LIKE THIS BIT…

BOOM!

WHAT WENT WRONG?

HE DRANK THE PETROL

5 Dad's Army is not all made up of older men. There are also boys too young to join the army. These fit young lads make good messengers. To make them even faster what does the LDV give the boys?

a) Motorbikes
b) Racing cycles
c) Roller skates

Answer:
c) There is a Home Guard section of 'Skating Boys' who can deliver help quickly by roller-skating to the place they are called!

NO TIME TO WAIT, I'VE GOT TO SKATE!

6 Dad's Army spend a lot of time practising shooting. Some become really good shots. One soldier manages to shoot down a German bomber over London. Amazing – but true.

7 Dad's Army are a bit like Boy Scouts. The Home Guard men can earn badges if they pass tests like map-reading and First Aid (which Scouts can do) … and bomb disposal (which Scouts don't do).

YOU'RE JOKING MATE! THAT'S A JOB FOR THE GIRL GUIDES!

BRAIN BLITZER

Is your brain brilliant? Or is it bomb-blitzed and banjaxed? Try this test on Blitzed Britain. Get more than nought out of ten and you are a Horrible Historian. Get less and you are probably a history teacher...

GLOOP!
GLOOP!

1 German submarines sink ships going to and from Blitzed Britain. But when they fire a torpedo at the cruise ship Arandora Star in July 1940 they make a big blitzed boob. Why?
a) The Arandora Star is made of rubber – the torpedo bounces back and sinks the German submarine.
b) The Arandora Star is full of Germans, not Blitzed Brits.
c) The Arandora Star is Adolf Hitler's favourite ship – he had cruised on her when he was a boy and he is very cross.

2 You haven't got a shelter and you haven't got a cellar. Bombs are falling. Quick, hide! Where?
a) Under the bed
b) Under the apple tree in the garden
c) Under the stairs

3 Of course the Brits must try to shoot down German bombers. You light up the skies with searchlights. You have barrage balloons on steel ropes to stop the bombers swooping low. You have gunners to fire cannon at them. So which is the most dangerous job?
a) on the searchlight
b) on the balloons
c) on the gun

4 Which Society helps to defeat enemy spies in Blitzed Britain?
a) The Boy Scouts for Freedom Society
b) The Spies and Secret Societies Society
c) The Golf, Cheese and Chess Society

5 A driver is caught speeding. He is driving at over 20 miles an hour at night. What sort of car is it?
a) A police car
b) A hearse carrying a corpse to a funeral
c) A doctor rushing to save a bomb victim

6 What are 'Pig Clubs' in Blitzed Britain?
a) A group of people who 'club' together to buy a piglet
b) Clubs for beating pigs
c) A group of people who dress like pigs to spy on pig farms

7 How can you use beer bottle tops to help the war?
a) Throw them at German bombers
b) Put them back on the beer bottles and save metal
c) Make them into jewellery

8 The government says EVERY single work place has to have a fire-watcher on guard at all times - to put out bomb fires as soon as they can. One place catches fire and there is no fire-watcher ready. Which place?
a) The Houses of Parliament - so the government breaks its own law
b) Buckingham Palace - so the King breaks the law
c) Cardiff Fire Station - so the fire station burns down

9 Two people in a car are killed when they are hit by...?
a) A ship
b) A chip
c) A whip

10 A man parachutes into your village. How do you check if he is a British pilot or a German?
a) Give him a word test - does he speak good English?
b) Give him a maths test - cunning Germans can do hard sums, like 37 times 54, in their heads.
c) Ask him to name his leader - if he says 'Hitler' shoot him. If he says 'Churchill' give him a cup of tea.

Answers on page 59

Where's Ratty? page 12

Rotten Roman Army Quiz page 18

1 b.

2 c (But they often barged straight down the middle of town streets in their chariots. They marched there too, trampling anyone who got in the way with their hob-nailed boots!).

3 a.

4 b (But they often had wives outside of the camp).

5 c.

6 b (But this rule was sometimes broken when the army was desperate for men ... and the men who were too small might still have to work for the army even if they couldn't fight).

7 a (And you'd share it with everyone else in the public toilets! Sometimes you'd use a lump of moss, though, and that would be flushed away).

8 a.

9 c.

10 b.

Nasty Normans page 23

1 True. He stumbled and fell forward as he reached the beach. Ooops! His men gasped. A bad sign. But witty Will grabbed some pebbles, stood up and said, 'See how I have grabbed England?'

2 True. It was another unlucky sign. William just laughed and said, 'This is the day I "turn" from Duke to King.'

3 False. William wore the bones of Saint Rasyphus and Saint Ravennus around his neck for luck.

4 True. The Normans didn't want to attack uphill and risk their lives. At 9 a.m. the minstrel Taillefer began to juggle with his sword and sing a battle song. He attacked – an English warrior moved forward to meet him and Taillefer lopped off his head. Taillefer moved on – the English shields parted to let him through where they hacked him down. He died.

5 True.

6 False.

7 False. Harold was *wounded* with an arrow to the eye. But he was *killed* when Norman knights charged forward and hacked him to bits.

8 False. Harold's face was smashed. Only his wife knew his corpse because she could spot its secret marks.

9 False. They said King Harold's corpse was taken to the sea shore and buried under a pile of stones. The English gave him a headstone reading, 'Harold, you rest here, to guard the sea and shore.'

10 True. The English told a story that Harold survived, buried under a pile of bodies. A peasant woman found him and nursed him back to health. He hid in a cellar in Winchester for two years before leading attacks on the hated Normans. In time he got religion and became Harold the hermit.

Mucky Manners page 27

1d; 2g; 3a; 4i; 5b; 6h; 7j; 8e; 9c; 10f

Scrambled Sayings page 29

1e); 2f); 3h); 4c); 5g); 6b); 7d); 8a)

And never forget, 'A Tyrone women will never buy a rabbit without a head for fear it's a cat.'

Spot the Lot! page 39

CHARLES II

NOT TOO MUCH I HOPE?

AWESOME ANSWERS

Spot the Lot! page 46

Brain Blitzer page 54

1 b. The Arandora Star is a cruise ship, not a warship, so the Germans should not have been firing at her. But she is painted grey so maybe the submarine captain thought it was a warship. The ship was taking German prisoners and German people to Canada. She sinks in 35 minutes. There are 1,500 people onboard and 800 die ... mainly Germans. Oooops!

2 c. Most German houses are built with cellars but Brit houses aren't, so the government says, 'You can always hide under the stairs'. It's good to be German at the start of the war, but later, when German cities are set ablaze by Brit bombers, the cellars become deadly. The fires suck all the air out of the cellars and the families suffocate. Not nice.

3 a. If the searchlight can see the bomber then the bomber can see the searchlight. Some enemy aircraft have the job of bombing the searchlights. It's dangerous there, standing next to your searchlight – if the bulb blows then so do you.

4 c. The 'Golf, Cheese and Chess Society' is the nickname for GCCS ... which is of course the 'Government Code and Cypher School' where spy-catchers learn to crack secret messages.

5 b. The undertaker is the first man to be fined for speeding. The corpse is late for her funeral. I don't think she'll mind too much.

6 a. A Pig Club is a group of people who 'club' together to buy a piglet. They feed it with all their food scraps. When it is nice and fat they kill it and eat it.

7 c. Yes, young ladies really do make jewellery from old beer bottle tops, cup hooks and corks.

8 a. On 10 May 1941, a bomb sets fire to the House of Commons. There is no one there to put it out.

Members of Parliament? Or Muppets in Parliament?

9 a. ... sort of.

When the Malakand is bombed it scatters itself over miles of Liverpool docks. A young couple are driving home along the dock road when bits of the ship land on their car and kill them.

They've just been married. Bride and boom.

10 a. Home Guards are given a list of words to see if a parachuting pilot can say them. Try them yourself:

Soothe Wrong Wretch Rats Those

One pilot who lands in Wapping, London, fails this test and is beaten to death. But he isn't a German enemy. He is a friendly pilot from Poland.

HORRIBLE HISTORIES
New Edition
MEASLY MIDDLE AGES
Splats, hats and lots of RATS!
Terry Deary
Illustrated by Martin Brown

HORRIBLE HISTORIES
New Edition
CUT-THROAT CELTS
Splats, hats and lots of RATS!
Terry Deary
Illustrated by Martin Brown

HORRIBLE HISTORIES
New Edition
GROOVY GREEKS
Splats, hats and lots of RATS!
Terry Deary
Illustrated by Martin Brown

HORRIBLE HISTORIES
New Edition
VILE VICTORIANS
Splats, hats and lots of RATS!
Terry Deary
Illustrated by Martin Brown

HORRIBLE HISTORIES
New Edition
TERRIFYING TUDORS
Splats, hats and lots of RATS!
Terry Deary
Illustrated by Martin Brown

HORRIBLE HISTORIES
OVER 200 STICKERS
TERRIFYING TUDORS
STICKER ACTIVITY BOOK
Terry Deary Illustrated by Martin Brown

HORRIBLE HISTORIES
WITH AWESOME 3 METRE FOLD-OUT TIMELINE
TERRIBLE TIMELINE
STICKER BOOK
Terry Deary Illustrated by Martin Brown
SEE HISTORY UNFOLD

HORRIBLE HISTORIES
THE BEASTLY BEST BITS
Terry Deary Illustrated By Martin Brown
I NEVER FORGET A FACE!

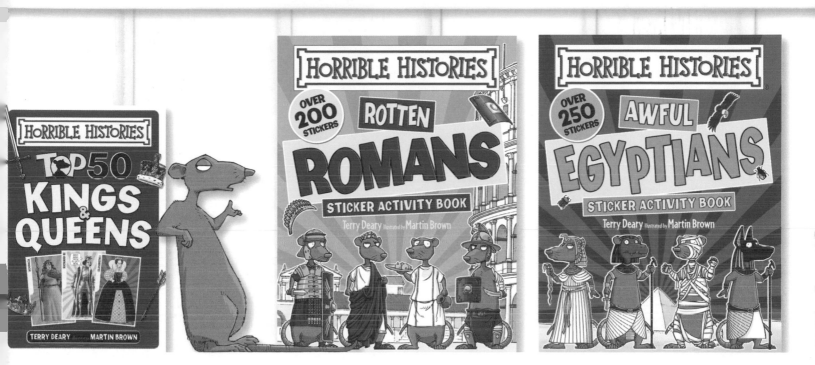